Viking Mead

The Honey Wine of Norse Mythology and Modern-Day Paganism

Preface

Are you someone who feels lost in the modern world?

Do you wish you could go back in time and live a simpler life where you're connected to nature?

There's no reason to keep living a life you don't enjoy. You only have one chance to make the most of it, and the Vikings knew that fact all too well. Asatru promotes bold thinking and strong actions. Brewing mead brings you closer to nature, and it's a simple process to learn. After reading this book, you will have all the tools you need to tackle life with the strength and fervor of an ancient Viking warrior.

Table of Contents

Introduction

Mead, also known as honey wine, is the oldest alcoholic drink in the history of the world. It was first discovered in 6500 BCE after ancient Northern Chinese farmers realized the honey produced by bees could be fermented into a beverage that would put a spring in their step. The cultivation of mead helped citizens of the ancient world get through long, cold winters, and its popularity quickly spread across the globe. It made its way to Europe between 2800 and 1800 BCE, becoming a popular drink with the native people of Northern Scotland, Ireland, and Scandinavia.

After mead arrived in Greece, it was considered potent enough to fuel the mythological beings of their pantheon, where it was etched into legends as ambrosia—the nectar of the gods. Ancient Rome did what Ancient Rome did best, creating a pale imitation of the Greek traditions. They spiced their wine with sweetened honey, offering the flavor of mead, but due to the base of the drink being fermented grapes, it wasn't true mead. The key that makes something true mead is the alcohol itself must come from honey, not merely have honey as a component.

The German and Irish Celts had the creation and consumption of mead intertwined with their culture. Chieftains were buried with large cauldrons filled with honey wine as an offering to the gods when their spirits passed over to the other side. Atop the Hill of Tara, where the ancient Irish kings were enthroned, the great mead hall known as *Tech Midchuarta* could hold up to 1,000 feasters, every single one of whom would have their cups overflowing with their favorite beverage.

As the ancient pagan religions developed, they drew upon the power of mead to use in their rituals. It was believed that honey wine could promote fertility and growth, making it especially popular in rituals centered around harvest festivals. Ancient pagans performed rites to pray for a bountiful yield when harvesting their crops and to thank the gods for their good fortune. They used mead in both rituals. Like the Greeks, they viewed mead as a drink worthy of their mythological deities. The use of alcohol in religious ceremonies was adopted by the Christians while attempting to convert the pagans, but they followed the Roman example, opting for wine from fermented grapes instead of mead.

The greatest purveyors of mead were the Vikings from Scandinavia. When it came to mead, they followed the "A, Bee, Sea" method—they aged the honey produced by bees in their apiaries and then carried it as it fermented while sailing across the seas. When they colonized a new land, the Vikings always had mead at the ready to celebrate their victories or drown their sorrows. The status of mead was such that it has become an enduring icon of the Viking age, the two inextricably linked by their shared travels around the world.

Chapter 1

The History of the Vikings

Vikings are known as some of history's fiercest warriors. Originating in Scandinavia during the 9th century CE, they spent around 200 years sailing the nearby seas to raid huge swathes of Europe and colonize neighboring lands. Viking warriors came primarily from Denmark, Norway, and Sweden, consisting of ancient pagans who carried their beliefs and traditions to the areas they conquered. Chief among their favorite libations was mead, which they brought with them on their long ships and fermented in the places they settled. This ensured they always had a steady supply of honey wine flowing from their cups to their bellies.

Who Were the Vikings?

While people tend to refer to Vikings as a catch-all term for warriors of 9th to 11th-century Nordic society, the true sense of the term is restricted to the collection of seafaring warriors who left their home countries and spent their time abroad. They were mostly made up of chieftains and the heads of clans who owned land, as well as their retainers, freemen, and any clan members with a taste for adventure and fortune. The most charismatic leaders recruited their clan's best young fighters to join them in seeking glory across the sea.

At home in their native lands, they were typically independent farmers or tradesmen; there were no professional armies, so warriors were required to seek other means to support themselves when no battles were fought. It was not unusual to see a man who could slice through enemy armies like they were butter-tilling, plowing their fields, wielding an iron sickle instead of a sword. They maintained gardens and orchards, raised livestock, and kept bees from which they harvested honey. That honey was used to create their mead.

Reasons for Leaving Home

There were some practical reasons why the Vikings set out on dangerous journeys across the sea to invade distant lands. By the turn of the 9th century, overpopulation was a problem in their home countries. Approximately 800,000 people were living in the area by 800 CE, and their population raced past 1 million in 1000

CE. There weren't enough local resources to sustain such a large number of individuals. Scandinavia was in danger of widespread hunger, famine, and violence between clans seeking control over the limited resources.

When the Nordic people looked at foreign countries, they saw lands with food and riches ripe for the taking. Scandinavian warriors were highly trained, brutal killing machines who could outmatch nearly any foe. The solution was obvious: send bands of warriors to plunder places with an overabundance of resources and establish colonies in those areas. Having a significant segment of their citizenry depart from Scandinavian shores would offer immediate relief to the overcrowding problem, and any resources the travelers returned with would boost their ability to sustain a thriving population.

How Vikings Operated

The Viking leadership gathered their warriors into warbands and sailed their longboats for England, Ireland, Greenland, Iceland, France, and Russia. Upon arriving at their destination, their first order of business was to raid settlements along the coast. They used hit-and-run tactics, invading a city or town and slaughtering its people, pillaging for food and treasure, and then burning everything in sight before departing. Due to their penchant for raiding and plundering, they earned their name—the term *Viking* was used in contemporary Scandinavian languages to mean "pirate."

The dense Nordic population allowed Viking armies to swell to vast sizes, and they became a fearsome foe for any foreign armies, who often had trouble fielding enough men to meet them in battle. However, with so many mouths to feed, Viking bands couldn't rely on looting alone. They began to establish their own colonies in the places they raided. From these initial settlements, Vikings launched campaigns of conquest, subduing local populations and taking control of kingdoms. The areas of Europe under attack by Vikings were left in a constant state of terror, never knowing when they could become the next target.

Conquest of England

After raiding the northern coasts of England, the Vikings set their sights on the rich kingdoms embroiled in fighting each other for more land. Danish Vikings led by three of Ragnar Lothbrook's sons—Halfdan, Ivar the Boneless, and Hubba—swarmed the northern kingdoms of England. Northumbria and East Anglia were conquered, while Mercia was decimated, leaving it a shadow of its former glory. Although they failed to conquer Wessex, they forced a truce with King Alfred the Great in 878. This truce led to a formal treaty in 886, in which Alfred officially recognized Danish dominion over most of England.

While the Vikings were pushed out of many English territories during the mid-10th century, they returned en masse in 980. England fell to the Viking threat in 1016. It was subsequently incorporated into the burgeoning empire of King Canute, a Danish prince who led the bulk of the Viking armies. Canute became King of Denmark two years later, followed in 1028 with his crowning as the King of Norway. At the height of his power, Canute was one of the most influential leaders in Europe. Canute's dynasty ended when William the Conqueror arrived from Normandy and took the throne in 1066, but the Vikings left an indelible mark on England that can be felt to this day.

Establishment of Normandy

Viking forces arrived in France during the reign of the Carolingian dynasty in the early 9th century. Unlike other destinations, the Carolingian Empire successfully repelled the invaders. However, at the beginning of 811, the Vikings sailed up the Seine River, raiding along the banks and setting up settlements around the lower Seine. These settlements became the seed that eventually grew into the Duchy of Normandy, and there was a significant Scandinavian influence on the development of Norman culture, including their language and institutions. When William the Conqueror rose to power and became the King of England, he brought Viking influences along with him.

Vikings in Ireland

Even before the Vikings invaded England, earlier groups sailed around the British Isles to raid Ireland. The first known landings took place in 795 when they pillaged numerous small islands off Ireland's northern and western coasts. By 840, they sailed inland along the rivers, targeting wealthy monasteries. Raiders plundered the monasteries and took captives who could be sold as slaves. Vikings created settlements in Dublin, Cork, Limerick, Waterford, and Wexford. The earliest Irish towns were built from the original Viking bases in these locations.

The Vikings also established trade routes through England and Continental Europe, in some cases reaching as far as the Byzantine Empire and Muslim-controlled Asia. Goods made from bronze, silver, gold, and other materials were sent out from Ireland along these trade routes, bringing in riches and helping to establish the country as a legitimate player on the world stage. Instead of being defeated in battle, the Vikings who colonized Ireland were converted to Christianity. They assimilated with the original native population, which is how the Irish became influenced by the Nordic customs.

Colonization of the North Atlantic

Bands of Vikings set out from Scandinavia to explore the North Atlantic, discovering Iceland, Greenland, and even North America. Iceland was colonized in 870, when Ingólfr Arnarson, a Viking chieftain from Norway, created the first permanent settlement in Reykjavík. An Icelandic explorer named Erik the Red set off with a Viking force in the late 10th century after he was exiled for murder, and he discovered Greenland in 982.

While sailing between Iceland and Greenland in 985, a Norwegian Viking captain named Bjarni

Herjólfsson was the first to encounter North America. After returning with tales of this distant new land, further expeditions were launched to settle it, including some led by Leif Erikson. The first ships sent to explore North America were led by Erikson, and he is believed to be the first European to step foot on American soil. This was about 500 years before famed explorer Christopher Columbus did the same. However, Erikson's contributions to the formation of modern North America never received the recognition enjoyed by the later "discovery."

Migration through Russia

When the Vikings reached Eastern Europe, they raided towns around the Baltic Sea, but the process was less extreme than it had been in Western Europe. They never established settlements in the area but managed to move deeper inland, migrating far into the heart of Russia. They intermingled with the local population, and this ethnic group became known as "Rus," a Scandinavian word that eventually gave Russia its name. The Rus people participated in trade with the Nordic countries and even attempted to emulate the Vikings by raiding neighboring lands.

During the first half of the 11th century, there was a second migration of Vikings into Eastern Europe. Swedish runic stones were erected that recorded the names of the Vikings who accompanied a chieftain named Yngvarr into the region, although records of their deeds are limited to semi-mythical accounts. Groups of Vikings offered their martial skills as mercenaries in the Byzantine Empire, traveling to the capital of Constantinople, where they formed the Varangian Guard. They were hired as bodyguards to protect the Byzantine emperors, becoming a version of the ancient Roman Praetorian Guard. The idea was that as foreign mercenaries, the Vikings would lack the political ambitions that turned the Praetorians into such a danger to the empire.

End of the Viking Age

By the time the 11th century ended, the problems that initiated the creation of Viking forces had largely ceased. The countries of Scandinavia were able to stabilize their populations and better manage their resources. England had long been severed from Denmark and Norway following the Norman conquest, and most Viking colonies were incorporated into local kingdoms.

Denmark, in particular, became a dominant power that established its own royal armies to conquer neighboring lands. The Norwegian king Olaf II Haraldsson is considered the last Viking chieftain, making the transition from a raider and pillager to a domestic leader when he was crowned in 1015.

Chapter 2

Mead: What It Is and Why It's Important

Viking warriors farmed the Nordic brown bee in their apiaries to produce honey for their mead. They were skilled farmers, knowledgeable in fermentation, and produced vast quantities of high-quality mead. When they held feasts, they did so in great mead halls built as reflections of Valhalla, Odin's own mead hall in Asgard. Drinking, eating, and celebrating were integral to Viking culture, with honey wine at its center.

How Honey Is Made

The creation of mead starts with bees. They pollinate flowers and collect nectar that they carry back to their hives. The nectar is broken down into base sugars, which are then stored within honeycombs and used as a food source. Bees require plenty of energy for flight, which they get through the honey they create. Honey also provides heat for the hive, keeping them warm through the cold winter months. Depending on the flower type the nectar is collected from, the resulting honey's color can range from a dark amber hue to a light yellow tint.

Most average beehives will make an excess of honey every year. This can be as much as 55 pounds of honey that goes unused by the hive. Beekeepers can harvest the extra honey by removing the wax on the honeycombs that keep the honey trapped in each cell. Modern beekeepers place the honeycomb frames into a centrifuge that forces the honey out, allowing them to collect it all into one place. Extracted honey is then strained to remove any bits of wax or dirt particles, purifying it for production and consumption. If the honey is not altered through additives like high fructose corn syrup, it can be sold as "pure" or "organic" honey.

The Fermentation Process

Once the honey has been extracted and purified, it can be used to create mead. To turn pure honey into honey wine, it has to be fermented with water and wild yeast. Many mead makers will flavor their beverage by adding spices, fruits, grains, or hops. Interestingly, the types of flowers that the bees have collected their nectar from also affects the taste of mead. Professional beekeepers control what kinds of flowers their bees use to make honey, allowing them to provide a particular flavor to mead production.

The fermentation process varies in length, but for the mead to reach the minimum requirement of alcohol content, it must be fermented for at least 10 to 20 days. During this time, it needs to be kept at a steady temperature of 70°F to 75°F (21.1°C to 23.9°C). Using additional ingredients and allowing it to ferment longer can result in a higher alcohol content, making the mead more potent to drink. As it ferments, the sugar in the mead is converted to alcohol, so more sugar can also give you a stronger beverage. However, to preserve the ability to call it "mead," honey must always be the primary ingredient providing that sugar. Most meads contain about 7.5% to 14% alcohol by volume (ABV).

What You Need to Make Mead

The great thing about mead is how easy it is to make on your own. You can find all the necessary materials around the house or buy them for a very low cost. Plenty of "do-it-yourself" kits also include everything you need to start brewing your own mead at home. Here's a quick list of the items you should have ready before you begin creating homemade mead:

Honey

Honey is the most important ingredient for making mead. The sugar in the honey is the primary component of the fermentation process, turning into alcohol as the mead is aged. Choosing the type of honey you use will affect the flavor of your brew, so decide early on how you want it to taste. You can add other ingredients to strengthen certain aspects of the flavor, but your honey will be the major influence on how it tastes. You can aim for something rich and sweet or dry with a bitter bite.

Water and Wild Yeast

Outside of honey, water and wild yeast are the only other two essential components to create mead. The water and yeast inject carbon dioxide into the brew and initiate fermentation by converting sugar particles into alcohol. The type of yeast used can change the consistency of your honey wine, making it thicker or thinner, depending on your preferences.

Fruits, Spices, and Other Flavoring

If you want to make your mead a bit more distinctive, add your blend of fruits, spices, grains, or other flavors. Some people add sugar to make their honey wine sweeter, while fruits like apples and bananas increase the sugar content of the brew. Lemons, oranges, or limes can give it a citrusy taste and cut through the sugar to make it less sweet. Including ginger, cloves, cinnamon, allspice, nutmeg, anise, cumin, or pepper offers the mead an interesting bite. Try playing around with different combinations to find the blend you like best.

Funnel

Funnels are one of the main pieces of equipment you need to brew mead. Anytime you move the brew around or add ingredients, using the funnel will prevent spills. The fermentation process requires carefully-measured portions of each ingredient so you know what to expect once the mead has aged. If the balance is thrown off because you lost too much while transferring your brew, you could end up with a bad-tasting batch of honey wine.

Demijohn

Demijohns are also known as carboys or Lady Janes. They are sturdy containers with a large body and narrow neck that can come in sizes between 1 to 16 gallons (4 to 60 liters) and can be made from plastic or glass. Some demijohns include a wicker casing that helps to protect the container, especially the ones made from glass. This is what you will use to actually ferment the mead.

Airlock, Bung, and Stopper

Airlocks are "S" shaped items that you attach to your demijohn to inject water into your fermenting mead. Bungs are rubber pieces that are used to attach the demijohns to the airlocks and look like a rubber stopper with a hole in the middle. These should allow you to place the tubing snugly, avoiding any spill-off. You will also need a fitted rubber stopper that can close the demijohn, preventing bacteria, microbes, and oxygen from getting into the mead and interfering with fermentation.

Tubing

You need a length of tubing to connect your airlock to the demijohn. It won't require much—a short piece measuring 5 or 6 inches (12.7 or 15.24 centimeters) is more than enough. Make sure the circumference of the tubing fits into your bung and can be attached securely to the airlock. This is where most spill-offs occur, and you don't want to have it leak water, as it will upset the balance during the fermentation process, resulting in less alcohol content and weaker flavor.

Food-Safe Bucket

A large food-safe bucket that can handle boiling water will be used to kick off the fermentation process. It needs to fit 2.5 to 3 gallons (9.5 to 11.4 liters) of liquid. There are plastic buckets made from high-density polyethylene plastic that are capable of safely containing boiling water at 248°F (120°C) for brief periods or up to 230°F (110°C) over longer periods. However, if you aren't sure whether your plastic bucket is made of this material, a metal food-safe bucket always works as a great vessel for boiling water.

Metal Spoon

You will need a large metal spoon to mix all the ingredients in your bucket. It should be big enough that you will get plenty of movement during the mixing process but not so big as to constantly be clanking against the sides while swirling the brew around. Spoons made from wood or heat-resistant materials can work as an alternative, but they have to be safe for use in boiling water. If your metal spoon doesn't have a handle, make sure you use protective gloves or oven mitts to keep from burning your hand.

Making Your Own Honey Wine

With all your equipment ready to go, you can start brewing your honey wine. You must keep everything sanitized to prevent unwanted bacteria and microbes from growing while fermenting. They thrive under the same conditions necessary to create the alcohol, and if any manage to sneak into your demijohn, it will ruin the entire batch. Just follow these simple steps to create your very own home-brewed mead:

Part I: Sterilization

1. Your yeast is the only thing you want to grow during the fermentation process. Every item used to brew your mead should be cleaned and sterilized before you begin. Wash your equipment and workspace with warm water and soap.

2. If you're using sanitization powder, fill your bucket with about 1.5 gallons (5.7 liters) of water, turning the powder into a sanitizing solution.

3. Add part of the sanitizing solution to your demijohn. Swirl the cleanser around, sanitizing the container. Pour the solution back into

your bucket, and make sure there is no residue remaining in your demijohn.

4. Place your funnel, bung, airlock, stopper, and spoon into the sterilizing solution in the bucket. Allow them to soak for several minutes.

5. Take the sterilized equipment out of your bucket and place them on your workspace. Set the funnel on top of your demijohn to ensure it doesn't touch any other surfaces that might contain bacteria or microbes.

6. Pour the sanitizing solution into the sink. Everything should be clean and prepared for the brewing process.

Part II: Brewing Process

These instructions are for brewing mead with a light ABV of about 4%. You can experiment with higher alcohol content in your brew once you're more familiar with the process.

1. Start with 500 grams of honey per gallon, which means 750 grams total for 1.5 gallons (about 132 grams of honey per liter for 5.7 liters).

2. Add 1.5 gallons (5.7 liters) of boiling water to your bucket.

3. Add the yeast (and acid regulator if necessary) to the bucket. Stir the mixture with your spoon until everything has dissolved.

4. Add your honey to the bucket and give it another stir. Make sure the honey has completely dissolved into the mixture.

5. Allow your brew to cool so it won't cause damage to your demijohn. Once it has cooled, use the funnel to transfer the brew from the bucket to the demijohn.

6. Continue to let the brew cool in the demijohn until it reaches room temperature of around 70°F to 75°F (21.1°C to 23.9°C).

7. Pitch the yeast by rehydrating it and allowing it to sit for 5 minutes. Add the yeast to your demijohn and gently shake it to mix everything together.

8. Attach the airlock to the demijohn using the length of tubing and bung. Fill the airlock with water and store it away in a dark, cool space. It should remain undisturbed for 10 to 20 days for the fermentation process to complete.

Part III: Fermentation, Back-Sweetening, and Conditioning

After combining all your ingredients and storing the brew away, you will have to perform some maintenance to complete the process. This mostly involves checking on your mead periodically to make sure it is fermenting properly and doing some additional work after the fermentation is complete.

1. If you have pitched the yeast correctly, you will notice gas beginning to bubble out of the airlock after approximately 6 hours. This is the carbon dioxide building up and escaping from the brew.

2. A layer of sediment will appear at the bottom of your demijohn during the fermentation process. This is a natural result of dead and dormant yeast. It won't harm your mead and can be skimmed off when your brew is ready.

3. After 14 to 18 days, the carbon dioxide bubbles will slow down and eventually cease to appear. At this point, you will know all the sugar has been converted into alcohol. It is almost ready for consumption.

4. Move your demijohn to the refrigerator for 24 to 48 hours. The cold temperature will cause the remaining yeast to become dormant and sink to the bottom. Keeping the brew in the fridge for a longer period of time will result in a clearer mead.

5. Siphon the top layer of your brew into your sanitized bucket using the tubing. However, don't transfer the sediment at the bottom of the demijohn with it. If you get your tubing within about 0.5 to 0.75 inches (1.27 to 1.9 centimeters) of the sediment, you can siphon the brew without getting any dormant yeast in the mix.

6. If you prefer mead that isn't too dry, back-sweeten it by adding more honey. To prevent the honey from fermenting further, you can use 2 Campden tablets. These are made of sodium metabisulphite, which kills bacteria and yeast.

7. Dissolve the honey and Campden tablets into a small amount of warm water and pour it into your fermented brew. Mix everything together until it has been completely dissolved.

8. Clean and sterilize your demijohn again, then transfer the mead back into it. Leave the

demijchn in direct sunlight at room temperature for 2 to 6 weeks in order to condition it. This allows the flavors to blend together and give your honey wine the best taste possible. If you have done everything correctly, you should have your very own home-brewed mead ready to drink. Feel free to share it with your family and friends!

Chapter 3

Asatru and Paganism

Asatru is a modern form of paganism heavily influenced by the rites, rituals, and beliefs of ancient Scandinavian and Germanic religions. They have adopted the religion practiced by the Vikings, resurrecting it for the modern age. Practitioners of Asatru are often called "heathens," and their neopagan religion is referred to as "heathenism" due to their belief system stemming from the days of pre-Christianity. The Asatruans wear that moniker like a badge of honor, displaying their devotion to the pagan gods of the Viking age.

The Evolution of Paganism

There were many pre-Christian cultures whose religion would qualify as paganism, but the term itself was first applied to civilians and non-combatants during the time of the Roman Empire. It is derived from the word *paganus*, which means "country dweller," "rustic," and "of the countryside." Early Christians throughout

Europe tended to take on words and phrases from the Roman military, and they began using "pagan" when referring to non-Christians exclusively.

Early Paganism and Christianity

In places like Scandinavia, Germany, France, and the British Isles, different forms of paganism thrived from prehistory to the Middle Ages. Celtic paganism was particularly popular, and the influence of the Celts was felt throughout Europe. Greece and ancient Rome were considered pagans, worshiping a polytheistic pantheon and establishing many cults and individual deities. The Nordic people had the Norse pantheon, which was spread across the Western world by the Vikings. These paganistic beliefs continue to influence the world today with the numerous neopagan and pagan revival religions.

Early pagan cultures were frequently in conflict with Christianity, especially as the latter religion grew in prominence. A common tactic was for the Christians to incorporate pagan rituals and traditions into the Christian religion. Christmas was celebrated right around the time of the winter solstice, which was a major festival in many forms of paganism. Saints and angels were associated with the pagan gods, giving them the same characteristics and dominions in order to appeal to the pagans and convince them to convert to Christianity.

Paganism in the British Isles

The Celts were the chief purveyors of paganism in the British Isles, with a heavy concentration in Scotland and Ireland. They worshiped gods such as Lugus, Cernunnos, Epona, Toutatis, Belenos, Maponos, Sucellos, Taranis, and Ogmios. Three was an important number to the Celtic pagans, which could be seen in the Matronae, or Three Mothers. Irish mythology had its own triple goddess in the Morrígan. They represented three different stages of life, expressed through the Maiden, the Mother, and the Crone.

During the time of the Roman invasion of Britain that started in 43 CE and lasted several centuries, the Roman gods accompanied the soldiers as they conquered the native Britons. While there were tribes of Celts and Picts who maintained their own religions, many of those living under Roman rule were converted to Roman paganism. Celtic paganism survived in Ireland and Scotland but was mostly wiped out in Britain. By the time the Romans departed, Angles and Saxons from Continental Europe landed on their shores, bringing their own belief systems.

Following the arrival of the Vikings, Anglo-Saxon paganism became the dominant religion in the British Isles. It had a Celtic flavor but took on many major aspects of Norse paganism, including the chief of their pantheon, Woden, also known as Odin. The Anglo-Saxons spread across the country and had a stranglehold on the religious character of the region, even managing to extinguish the first glimmers of Christianity until the Norman Invasion. Once the Normans had taken over England, they transformed the country from a haven of paganism to a kingdom of Christianity.

Germanic and Norse Paganism

Germanic paganism evolved out of the early Indo-European polytheistic religions. In addition to a pantheon of gods, they believed in giants, elves, dwarfs, dragons, and other mythological creatures. In other areas of Europe, Germanic paganism branched off into various forms, including Norse paganism in Scandinavia. Norse paganism retained many of the core beliefs of Germanic paganism but codified a pantheon and mythology that would later travel beyond Scandinavia with the Vikings.

At the center of the Norse cosmology was Yggdrasil, a massive ash tree that connected the Nine Worlds. Each world was inhabited by real and mythological beings of Norse paganism, such as Asgard, the world of the Aesir gods; Jotunheim, where the giants dwelled; Niflheim, a world of primordial ice; Muspelheim, Niflheim's opposite, a place of primordial fire; Vanaheim, home to the Vanir gods; Alfheim, the elvish world; Svartalfheim, the land of the dwarfs; Hel, where the dead reside; and Midgard—our world.

When the Vikings set off to explore, raid, and colonize new lands, they continued praying to the same gods and performing the same rituals as they had done at home. They were fiercely loyal to their pagan beliefs, absolutely certain that their sacrifices, offerings, and rites swayed the favor of their deities. If the oceans they were sailing on rose up, trapping them in turbulent waters, it was because they had somehow offended Njord, god of the sea. When their battles went well, they thanked Tyr, the god of war, for lending his power to their sword arms. This reverence and attention to tradition was lost when Christianity overtook paganism as the primary religion of Western Europe. These days, there have been efforts to revive Viking ideals and religion.

Modern Paganism

While it's rare to find an unbroken line of pagan heritage that stretches back to before the rise of Christianity, there are many neopagan religions that have taken up the beliefs of ancient paganism. Wicca, which was established around the middle of the 20th century, is a nature-focused religion that draws from various pagan traditions of the past. Modern Druidry mimics ancient Druidism that was once prominent in Celtic society. Shamanism invokes the form of paganism practiced by indigenous peoples native to Africa and the Americas.

Asatru

Of all the Neopagan religions, Asatru hews most closely to their forebears. They have adopted many traditions, rituals, and beliefs propagated by the medieval Germanic pagans, particularly Norse pagans. It was founded in 1972 by Sveinbjörn Beinteinsson, an Icelandic sheep farmer who gathered together 11 like-minded people to bring back the traditions of Norse paganism. Asatru slowly gained traction throughout the latter part of the 20th century, becoming a popular religion in Iceland and beyond. By 2013, Asatru had practitioners in 98 countries and could claim over 40,000 devotees.

The name *Asatru* stems from an Old Norse word meaning "faith in the Aesir." The Aesir were the most prominent tribe of gods in Norse paganism. Their numbers included Odin, the chief of both the Aesir and the Norse pantheon as a whole; Frigg, Odin's wife; Thor, the god of thunder and son of Odin and Frigg; and Baldr, the invulnerable brother of Thor, who served as the god of peace, joy, and light. It was the Aesir who brought an end to the terrible wars between them and the Vanir, another tribe of gods. To help broker this peace, the Vanir siblings, known as Freyr and Freya, joined the Aesir in their home of Asgard.

Asatruars seek to emulate the Vikings in their belief system. They maintained the values propagated by those who practiced Norse paganism. Like their predecessors, practitioners of this neopagan religion have certain ideals they strive to embody. The core tenets of Asatru are known as the Nine Noble Virtues. These include:

1. Courage
2. Truth
3. Honor
4. Fidelity
5. Discipline
6. Hospitality

7. Self-reliance

8. Industriousness

9. Perseverance

Holding to these values encourages Asatruars to live a better life. Like the Vikings of old, you must follow these tenets in everything you do. A life without them isn't a life worth living. No matter your task, activity, or job, you must never stray from the Nine Noble Virtues. They penetrate your very being and allow you to become the best version of yourself.

When Vikings broke their oaths, they were punished by the goddess Vár. She was responsible for holding Vikings to their vows. When they became oathbreakers, Vár was invoked to bring swift justice upon their heads. While modern neopagans like Asatruars might not be as bloodthirsty when meting out punishment, you can expect to be shunned by your community or excommunicated from participating in any religious activities. The spirit of Vár remains strong in how there is zero tolerance for those who would break the Nine Noble Virtues and cause harm to others.

Chapter 4

Important Feasts of the Runic Era Calendar

Asatru practitioners observe the runic era calendar like the Vikings and other Germanic pagans. It remained in use throughout Northern Europe until the 19th century, when it fell out of favor and was replaced by the Gregorian calendar. However, Asatru has revived it and uses it to mark their feasts, festivals, and holidays. The runic era calendar also has its own names for the months, which are given as the following:

1. January=*Snowmoon*
2. February=*Horning*
3. March=*Lenting*
4. April=*Ostara*
5. May=*Merrymoon*
6. June=*Midyear*
7. July=*Haymoon*
8. August=*Harvest*
9. September=*Shedding*

10. October=*Hunting*

11. November=*Fogmoon*

12. December=*Yule*

High Feast of Yule

Unlike the Gregorian calendar, which starts its year on January 1, the runic era calendar begins on 22 *Yule* (December 22). That is when they celebrate the High Feast of Yule, which is right around the winter solstice and the shortest day of the year. It is considered sacred to the gods Thor and Freya, who are honored during the Yuletide celebrations. The festival lasts for 12 days, and on 31 *Yule* (December 31), culminating in the apt-ly-named Twelfth Night celebration. Asatruars swear oaths for the upcoming year on Freya's boar or their own hammers.

Charming of the Plow

The Charming of the Plow is an agricultural ritual on 3 *Snowmoon* (January 3). Baked goods like bread and cakes or grains are given as offerings to promote soil fertility in the upcoming year. You should crumble the offering and spread it out on the earth while invoking the names of Odin and Frigg to heal the land and keep it safe. This blessing ensures a successful growing season with healthy, hearty crops.

Feast of Vali

The Feast of Vali is celebrated on 14 *Horning* (February 14), and coincides with the Christian and secular holiday of Valentine's Day. It honors the legend of Vali, a son of Odin who sprung from his father and grew to manhood within a single day. He was born for the sole purpose of slaying Hodr in revenge for the death of Baldr after Loki tricked Hodr into killing his brother with a mistletoe spear. Baldr was invulnerable to all weapons save those made from mistletoe, and Hodr was unaware that his weapon was made from it when Baldr challenged him to strike him. The Feast of Vali also celebrates the return of the sunlight after a dark, cold winter. It is a time for family and love—many marriages and vow renewals take place on this day.

High Feast of Ostara

The High Feast of Ostara takes place on the spring equinox, usually around 20 *Lenting* (March 20). This is a time of renewal, and the festival celebrates new growth and rebirth. You can perform the Blot ritual to honor Freya, Frigg, and Nerthus. In addition, pour a libation of mead onto the earth to promote the growth of crops, plants, and flowers.

Yggdrasil Day

Yggdrasil Day falls on 22 *Ostara* (April 22), a day to honor Yggdrasil's role in the universe. You can reflect on how Yggdrasil has influenced Asatru heritage, culture, and spirituality. All life sprung from the limbs of the great world tree, and it will provide refuge to the inhabitants of the Nine Worlds following Ragnarök. To celebrate Yggdrasil's gifts to mankind, plant a tree in its name. Nurture this tree year-round and protect it as it grows to be a mighty child of Yggdrasil.

May Day

May Day is a festival extending well beyond Asatru, celebrated across Europe on 1 *Merrymoon* (May 1). By this point in the year, nature is in bloom, resulting in deep green grass fields that flourish with colorful flowers. The leaves on the trees have returned, filling out the bare winter branches. Freya is the patron goddess of May Day, so venerate her with prayers and gifts.

Midsummer

Midsummer is celebrated around the summer solstice, which is also the longest day of the year. It takes place on 21 *Midyear* (June 21), marking the halfway point of the runic era calendar. Asatruars give thanks for the victory of the sun in its battle against darkness. Since the sun is associated with Baldr, he is the god who is honored during the festival of Midsummer. Perform a Blot dedicated to him and celebrate with a grand feast and a cold glass of mead.

Founder's Day

Founder's Day is unique to the Asatru runic era calendar. Falling on 4 Haymoon (July 4), practitioners follow the lead of the United States in celebrating their Founding Fathers by honoring the founders of Asatru. Give thanks on this day to Australian H. Rud Mills, Icelander Thorsteinn Guthjonson, and the central figure of Asatru, Sveinbjörn Beinteinsson. It's a day when you can reflect on the sacrifices and staunch dedication to Asatru displayed by its founders, as well as consider what the religion means to you and how you can help promote its growth in the future.

Alvablot

Celebrated on 26 *Harvest* (August 26), Alvablot is a festival honoring Odin, Freya, and the elves of Alfheim. You should perform a Blot ritual for them on this day to give thanks for the fertility of the land and women. Traditionally, women would lead the Blot, as it is a feminine holiday. It is customary to offer mead or beer to the gods and elves during Alvablot celebrations.

Winter Finding

Winter Finding coincides with the autumn equinox, which occurs around 23 *Shedding* (September 23). This is the day when the summer and winter are in balance, having an equal amount of day and night. You Dedicate a Blot to Odin, asking him for strength in surviving the lean days of winter when food and merriment become scarce. It can be the last chance to enjoy the nice weather before the onset of the frosty winter and longer nights.

Vetrablot/Winter Nights

On 14 *Hunting* (October 14), Asatru practitioners celebrate Vetrablot, also known as Winter Nights. It is the day when the female spirits known as the Disir are venerated, while Freya is also given blessings and thanks for the bountiful harvest. You can perform a Blot ritual for Freya and the Disir, making an offering to show your appreciation for their protection. In addition, pour a libation of mead, ale, or milk onto the land as thanks for the gifts of the earth itself.

Feast of the Einherjar

The Einherjar are the chosen warriors who serve Odin and feast in the halls of Valhalla until they are needed to fight during Ragnarök. These warriors are the souls of our ancestors who fought and died to protect their loved ones. The Feast of the Einherjar takes place on 11 *Fogmoon* (November 11). It is a time to thank them for their service and sacrifice—if you have any deceased kin who fought and died in battle, visit their graves and pour a libation of mead in their honor. Alternatively, drink a libation of mead in their memory if you cannot visit their graves in person.

Mother Night

Mother Night takes place on 21 *Yule* (December 21) and marks the final day of the runic era calendar. Thor and Freya are honored on Mother Night with a Blot, Sumbel, and preparations for the High Feast of Yule the next day. Reflect on the past year and take measure of everything for which you should be grateful. You can burn a Yule log and leap over it to purify your spirit and bring you good luck in the New Year.

Chapter 5

Rituals and Rites of Asatru

Part I: Blot

Blót is an Asatru ritual where a gift is offered to the gods after the gift itself has been made sacred. It was considered one of the most important rituals in Germanic paganism prior to the advent of Christianity. Even the early Christian kings in Scandinavia honored the Blot rituals to maintain support from the pagan tribes. The term *blot* comes from an Old Norse word that means "sacrifice." As such, the point of the ritual is to sacrifice something important to the gods, proving your devotion to them. In order to complete the ritual of Blot, you must first sanctify an item worthy as an offering.

What You Need for Blot

- An item to serve as your gift. The most common types of gifts offered during Blot are food and beverages. These can include:

- ○ Mead, wine, beer, or other spirits
- ○ Whole grains like wheat, oats, barley, and rye (they can be raw or cooked into a porridge)
- ○ Baked goods like bread, cakes, pies, and pastries.
- ○ Fresh or dried fruits like apples, pears, lemons, grapes, oranges, and limes
- ○ Wild or cultivated flowers
- ○ Tree or seed nuts
- ○ Products made from animals, like cheese and butter
- ○ Effigies of animals like bears, wolves, deer, sheep, goats, and cows
- An offering of mead for libation (separate from the gift)
- A bowl to catch some of the libation to perform a blessing
- A sprig of evergreen for aspersion
- Water and fire to bless and purify your gift and holy space
  - ○ You need a brazier or fire pit for your sacrificial fire, but you can also include candles or torches

○ Bring the water in a clean bowl, jug, or other similar vessel to wash your hands and face prior to touching the gift

Making Your Offering

When making an offering to the gods, your gift to them needs to be made holy so it can pass over from our world to the world of the gods. To do this, follow these instructions:

1. Set up your source of fire (a brazier or fire pit) in your holy space, using wood or an accelerant if necessary.
2. Fill your bowl, jug, or other vessel with fresh water.
3. Collect everyone's offerings if performing Blot with others.
4. Gather all participants together for a procession into your holy space.
5. Distribute any candles or torches being used for the ritual.
6. Light the candles or torches before proceeding to your holy space.
7. Walk 3 laps around your holy space while holding the lit candles or torches, chanting a prayer for blessing and purification.

8. Light the sacrificial fire.

9. Wash your face and hands with the fresh water, then pour it out when you're done.

10. Recite a prayer to invoke the gods and goddesses of your choice, sanctifying your offerings.

11. Pour out your libation of mead and catch a portion in your bowl for the blessing.

12. Place the offerings into the sacrificial fire or set them down upon a sacred altar or stone.

13. Kneel or prostrate yourself before the sacrificial fire.

14. With the gifts blessed and offerings made, give a blessing to all participants before leaving the holy space.

Part II: Sumbel

Sumbel is a rite that includes sitting around with friends, family, and members of your community, passing a horn of mead, and making boasts, toasts, and oaths to honor the gods and each other. It is typically performed after completing the Blot ritual, serving as a sort of counterpoint. Blot is about sacrifice and offering a gift to the gods, while Sumbel is about celebration of the gifts given by the gods to you.

Performing a Sumbel

In order to perform a Sumbel, follow these steps:

1. Gather together the participants somewhere indoors. A hall or dining space is ideal, somewhere big enough for everyone to participate.

2. Arrange the participants into a circle or rectangle. A Viking Sumbel included a "high seat" at the head of the hall for the chieftain or clan leader. You can give this seat to a venerable group member or forgo the high seat entirely.

3. Fill your horn or drinking vessel with mead. This act signifies the official beginning of the Sumbel. The leader or a respected group member can bless or pray while the horn is filled.

4. Give a toast to the gods, starting with an address to your chosen gods or goddesses, such as "Hail Odin" or "Hail Freya." You can recite a longer toast or verse from a Viking skald. The person giving the toast will take a sip from the horn, and the other participants should reply by saying, "Hail!"

5. Pass the horn around to the other participants. You can do this by handing it to the person next

to you, going around the entire ring or rectangle until everyone has sip. You can also designate someone as the official horn-bearer, and they will hand the horn to each participant in turn and then receive it before moving on to the next person.

Roles of the Sumbel

Every Sumbel assigns special roles to chosen individuals for them to perform during the rite. These roles include:

- **The Thul**: This is someone who knows each participant well. The Thul is meant to challenge any boasts containing untruths or exaggerations. When someone takes an oath, the Thul makes those swearing it define their oath. This prevents the person from being able to avoid their oath through a technicality. The Thul also acts as a sort of sergeant-at-arms, stepping in when things get too rowdy or combative, ejecting uncooperative participants, or shutting the Sumbel down if the situation becomes dangerous.

- **The Shope**: They are a bard, singer, or poet who recites verses concerning the gods, heroes, and ancient myths enshrined in legend. In addition, they can offer songs or poems recounting great deeds performed by participants of the Sumbel. Their role is to get everyone in the right headspace for the rite and pass on historical and religious knowledge in an easily digestible manner.

- **The Horn-Bearer**: They are assigned to handle and carry the drinking horn throughout the Sumbel. When someone is designated the Horn-Bearer, no participant is permitted to pass the horn directly to anyone else besides the Horn-Bearer. This position of honor should be given to someone who has earned the respect of everyone involved in the rite.

Part III: Profession

Profession is an essential ceremony in Asatru. It involves professing your belief in the gods and your kinship with fellow practitioners. Profession often serves as a turning point in a person's religious journey and the beginning of an awakening to better understand yourself. It is a relatively short ceremony compared to Blot and Sumbel. However, that doesn't diminish the significance of Profession. It is the most intimate of the rituals, as you are the only person who declares devotion to the gods.

Completing Profession

A Gothi will help you perform the ceremony. It can take place directly before or after the Blot ritual. To complete the ritual, follow these directions:

1. The ceremony begins with the Gothi standing in front of the altar. They will say, "Will [your name] please step forward?"

2. Walk over to the Gothi, facing them while standing before the altar. They will say, "Are you here of your own free will? Is it your intention to solemnly swear allegiance and kinship to the gods of Asgard—the Aesir and Vanir?"

3. Answer yes to both questions. The Gothi will pick up an oath ring or alternative sacred object for you to swear your oath upon.

4. When the Gothi holds out the object, grasp it and repeat this phrase when prompted: "I swear to ever uphold the Raven Banner of Asgard, to follow the way of the North, to always act with honor and bravery, and to be ever true to the

Aesir and Vanir and Asatru. By the gods, I so swear. By my honor, I so swear. On this Holy Ring, I so swear. Hail the gods."

5. If anyone else is present, they will repeat "Hail the gods" once you are finished reciting your oath.

6. The Gothi completes the ceremony by saying, "Then be welcome to the service of Asgard and the community of Asatru."

Part IV: Recipes for Offerings

When making your offerings during the rituals, rites, and ceremonies, you can use different recipes for the food and beverages to personalize them. Creating your own variation on standard offerings can help show the gods that you are willing to put in the extra effort and ensure your gifts to them prove the depths of your devotion. Here are some ideas for specialized recipes to get you started:

Spiced Winter Mead

Spiced Winter Mead has a mildly sweet flavor and a rich, complex blend of spices that adds warmth and bite to your brew. It is perfect for rituals undertaken during the coldest months of the year. This recipe will yield 5 gallons (19 liters) of mead.

Ingredients:

- 20 pounds (9.07 kilograms) of honey from blackberry, orange, or raspberry blossoms
- 5 gallons (19 liters) of water
- 7 grams (1.4 teaspoons) of ground nutmeg
- 7 grams (1.4 teaspoons) of ground cinnamon
- 7 grams (1.4 teaspoons) of dried ground ginger
- 1 gram (0.2 teaspoon) of ground cloves
- 1 small vanilla bean

Yeast:

- 15 grams (3 teaspoons) of rehydrated yeast (for best results, use yeast 1056 or Lalvin 71B-1122)

8 to 12 hours after yeast has pitched:

- 4 grams (0.8 teaspoon) of diammonium phosphate (DAP)
- 3 grams (0.6 teaspoon) of Fermaid K

Over the next 3 days, add once per day:

- 2 grams (0.4 teaspoon) of DAP
- 2 grams (0.4 teaspoon) of Fermaid K

Instructions:

1. Mix all the ingredients together and aerate them thoroughly by using an immersion blender or kitchen mixer.

2. Stir each additional ingredient well to de-gas your brew.

3. After fermentation has finished (21 to 28 days for most yeast, 24 to 30 days for Wyeast 1056), transfer the brew to a secondary container.

4. Allow the brew to age for 6 to 12 months.

5. Use Sparkolloid to help clear the mead completely if necessary. Follow the instructions included with the product.

6. Rack the brew again to reduce the amount of sediment in your final brew.

7. Once fermentation has completely ceased, you can fill empty bottles with the mead.

Honey Wine Bread

If you want an offering that combines two traditional items given to the gods, Honey Wine Bread is the perfect recipe. It is a spin on beer bread, resulting in a final product that's denser and sweeter. This recipe yields one loaf (six servings) of Honey Wine Bread.

Ingredients:

- 3 cups of sifted flour
- ¼ cup of honey
- 12 ounces of mead

- ½ cup of melted unsalted butter (use ¼ cup for a less crunchy crust)
- 3 teaspoons of baking powder (if not using self-rising flour)
- 1 teaspoon of salt (if not using self-rising flour)

Instructions:

1. Preheat your oven to 375°F (190.6°C).
2. Combine the dry ingredients and mix well, then add in the honey mead.
3. Grease a loaf pan with butter and pour in the mixture.
4. Drizzle the melted butter evenly over the dough.
5. Bake for 60 minutes, until the crust is golden brown.
6. Remove the pan from your oven and let it cool before serving.

Hot Mead Toddy

The Hot Mead Toddy gives you a warm, soothing drink that can help you relax before performing a ritual. It also makes for a great offering, as not even the gods would say no to this delicious hot beverage. Since it is relatively simple and quick to make, you can whip one up fast anytime you want. This recipe yields 4 servings of Hot Mead Toddy.

Ingredients:

- 1.5 ounces (0.44 liter) of traditional mead
- 1 ounce (0.3 liter) of rye whiskey
- 1 teaspoon of honey
- 1 slice of fresh ginger
- 1 slice of lemon
- 1 cup (0.24 liter) of water

Instructions:

1. Pour the water into a saucepan or teapot and bring it to a simmer
2. Transfer the hot water to mugs
3. Add the mead, whiskey, and honey to the hot water, then mix it thoroughly
4. Garnish with fresh ginger and lemon slice

Conclusion

Vikings and mead are very important to Asatru and other forms of neopaganism. They have brought back the belief system formerly seen across Western Europe. The Vikings spread their particular brand of paganism far and wide, but it was eventually superseded by other religions, like Christianity, Islam, Judaism, Buddhism, and Hinduism. However, the Neopagan movement has pulled ancient pagan religions from the history books and revived them in the modern world.

A rich tradition and heritage connects Asatru to the Vikings and ancient pagans. Honoring the gods through rituals, feasts, and offerings promotes a sense of oneness between you and the universe. Respect for nature and preserving the natural world are aspects of neopaganism that coincide with the recent popularity of an eco-friendly ethos promoted by secular society. Becoming a member of Asatru means helping to stop mankind's encroachment upon the rapidly shrinking countryside and wilderness.

The veneration of nature by pagans and Vikings has a direct line to the activities of modern pagans like the Asatruars. Vikings cultivated bees on their farms at home, using the honey produced by the bees to brew mead. It can be made with all-natural ingredients, including yeast created from grains and collected from fruits or vegetables. Mead is such a simple beverage to brew and has a variety of flavors to suit your tastes. You can drink your honey wine, of course, as the Vikings did during their celebrations held in great mead halls. However, it can also serve as an excellent offering to the gods during rituals and festivals.

All pagan rituals share a common theme: sacrificing to prove your devotion. By giving up something you took the time and effort to create, you show your willingness to yield the product of your own labor in exchange for the blessings of your deities. Asatru rituals and rites combine this ideal and joyous celebration of life and the world around you. As much as you are expected to make sacrifices, you're also meant to take pleasure in the fruits of your labor. You can make an offering with your mead and then share the rest with your friends, family, and fellow Asatruars.

Everything that connects the Vikings to Neopagans comes from the desire to rise above society's current problems. The Vikings first left their homelands because the populace needed a release valve to avoid overcrowding and starvation. They set out on their journeys, not knowing what to expect in the lands they found. While they could be brutal to the native peoples they encountered, they also expanded many cultures and significantly influenced the places where they settled. Just like the Vikings found a novel solution to their people's troubles, you can use the lessons and values of Asatru to create a better life and help to improve society as a whole.

References

Bhaerman, B. (2015, February 6). *Paganism*. AHA - American Humanist Association. https://americanhumanist.org/wp-content/uploads/2016/11/paganism.pdf

Boeckmann, C. (2023, November 16). *Beekeeping 101: How to Start Raising Bees – Planning | The Old Farmer's Almanac*. Www.almanac.com. https://www.almanac.com/beekeeping-101-getting-started-planning-for-bees

Dougall, D. M. (2014). *Viking treasure: The buzz about liquid gold*.

Elly, M. (2019, March 16). *Vár: The norse keeper of vow that punished oath breakers*. BaviPower. https://bavipower.com/blogs/bavipower-viking-blog/var-the-keeper-of-promise

Gosnell, T. (2021, January 27). *How to make mead*. BBC Good Food. https://www.bbcgoodfood.com/howto/guide/how-to-make-mead

Hellquist, E., & Robarts - University of Toronto. (1922). Svensk etymologisk Ordbok. In *Internet Archive*. Lund, Gleerup. https://archive.org/details/svensketymologis00hell/page/668/mode/2up

Hengest. (2009, May 25). *The nine noble virtues and charges of the Odinic Rite*. The Odinic Rite - Odinism for the Modern World. https://odinic-rite.org/main/the-nine-noble-virtues-and-charges-of-the-odinic-rite/

Jereme Zimmerman. (2015). *Make mead like a viking : traditional techniques for brewing natural, wild-fermented, honey-based wines and beers*. Chelsea Green Publishing.

Kendrick, T. D. (2014). *A history of the Vikings*. Routledge, Taylor & Francis Group.

Knut Helle, Kouri, E. I., & Olesen, J. E. (2003). *The Cambridge history of Scandinavia*. Cambridge University Press.

Mawer, A. (Allen), & The Library of Congress. (1913). The vikings. In *Internet Archive*. Cambridge [Eng.] The University press. https://archive.org/details/vikings00mawe

McCoy, D. (2012, November 15). *The nine worlds*. Norse Mythology for Smart People. https://norse-mythology. org/cosmology/the-nine-worlds/

National Honey Board. (2017, June 11). *How honey is made*. National Honey Board. https://honey.com/ about-honey/how-honey-is-made

Peterson, G. D. (2016). Vikings and Goths: A History of Ancient and Medieval Sweden. In *Google Books*. McFarland. https://books.google. com/book s?id=joawDAAAQBAJ&pg=PA203#v= onepage&q&f=false

Salem Media. (2014, June 8). *Viking farms: What was life on the farm like?* History on the Net. https://www. historyonthenet.com/life-on-a-viking-farm

Stead, L. (2007, November 18). *Rituals of Asatru*. Ravenbok. https://www.ravenkindred.com/Ravenbok. html

The Asatru Alliance. (2010, February 18). *asatru.org*. The Asatru Alliance. https://www.asatru.org/holidays.php

The National Museum of Ireland. (2020, July 16). *The viking age in Ireland*. National Museum of Ireland.

https://www.museum.ie/en-IE/Collections-Research/Irish-Antiquities-Division-Collections/Collections-List-(1)/Viking/The-Viking-Age-in-Ireland

The Troth. (2023, May 11). *Rituals*. The Troth. https://thetroth.org/resources/rituals/

Thor's Oak Kindred. (2017, June 24). *Ásatrú*. Thor's Oak Kindred. https://www.thorsoak.info/p/asatru.html